EP High School
Biology Printables:
Levels 9-12

This book belongs to:

_____

This book was made for your convenience. It is available for printing from the Easy Peasy All-in-One Homeschool website. It contains all of the printables from Easy Peasy's High School Biology course. The instructions for each page are found in the online course. THIS BOOK IS NOT A COMPLETE COURSE. The rest of the course is found online.

Easy Peasy All-in-One Homeschool is a free online homeschool curriculum providing high quality education for children around the globe. It provides complete courses for preschool through high school graduation. For EP's curriculum visit allinonehomeschool.com.

EP High School Biology Printables: Levels 9-12

ISBN: 9798324488826

First Edition: May 2024

Grading Sheet: Quarter 1

Biology with Lab

Record your scores on the sheet below as the assignments instruct you to do so.

Date	Lesson	Assignment	My Score	Possible Score
	2	Assignment		10
	5	Assignment		30
	6	Questions		4
	7	Quiz		8
	9	Experiment		15
	10	Quiz		7
	11	Assignment		6
	11	Paragraph		5
	12	Questions		4
	12	Assignment		10
	13	Assignment		20
	14	Questions		5
	15	Questions		15
	16	Questions		5
	17	Assignment		5
	18	Assignment		5
	20	Questions		20
	20	Quiz		10
	21	Questions		3
	24	Two quizzes		28
	27	Lab		20
	29	Quiz		10
	29	Project		20
	30	Test		20
	31	Questions		2
	31	Project		10
	33	Questions		15
	36	Test		25
	38	Questions		25
	40	Assignment		15
	44	Questions		10
	44	Assignment		20
	45	Lab		12
		TOTAL		

Grading Sheet: Quarter 2

Record your scores on the sheet below as the assignments instruct you to do so.

Date	Lesson	Assignment	My Score	Possible Score
	47	Paragraph		5
	48	Quiz		6
	48	Assignment		8
	50	Test		24
	51	Assignment		20
	53	Assignment		35
	54	Questions		8
	55	Lab		10
	58	Assignment		10
	59	Questions		6
	60	Lab		16
	61	Assignment		8
	61	Assignment		5
	62	Assignment		28
	63	Questions		19
	64	Test		20
	67	Questions		4
	71	Lab		50
	72	Questions		23
	74	Questions		24
	77	Two quizzes		20
	83	Questions		17
	84	Lab		20
	85	Questions		3
	85	Assignment		10
	87	Questions		15
	88	Two quizzes		20
	89	Questions		10
		TOTAL		

Grading Sheet: Quarter 3

Record your scores on the sheet below as the assignments instruct you to do so.

Date	Lesson	Assignment	My Score	Possible Score
	94	Problems (extra credit possible)		15
	95	Assignment		20
	96	Assignment		10
	97	Assignment		25
	99	Lab		24
	103	Lab		24
	104	Two quizzes		15
	107	Assignment		28
	108	Assignment		10
	111	Assignment		10
	111	Assignment		12
	112	Assignment		13
	113	Assignment		6
	117	Paragraph		5
	120	Project		50
	120	Quiz		8
	121	Lab		38
	125	Presentation		30
	127	Paragraph		10
	128	Assignment		5
	129	Questions		15
	130	Assignment		35
	130	Quiz		10
	135	Answer		5
		TOTAL		

Grading Sheet: Quarter 4

Record your scores on the sheet below as the assignments instruct you to do so.

Date	Lesson	Assignment	My Score	Possible Score
	143	Test		10
	144	Assignment		17
	145	Assignment		10
	146	Lab		11
	147	Assignment		20
	148	Assignment		12
	148	Assignment		10
	149	Quiz		10
	152	Assignment		12
	154	Lab		50
	155	Paragraph		10
	157	Lab		10
	159	Assignment		24
	160	Quiz		12
	163	Lab		20
	164	Questions		27
	165	Assignment		20
	167	Lab		24
	168	Assignment		25
	172	Questions		14
	177	Lab		25
	179	Lab		20
	180	Final exam		100
		TOTAL		

Lesson 1: Key Terms

Subdivisions of Biology (including but not limited to)

Anatomy: the structure of organisms

Bacteriology: bacteria

Botany: plants

Cytology: cells and how they work

Ecology: the relationship between living things and their environment

Ophthalmology: eyes and diseases of the eye

Pathology: diseases

Physiology: functions of organisms, organs, tissues, cells, organelles, etc.

Radiology: what x-rays reveal about living things

Virology: viruses

Branches of Biology specifically related to animals

Apiarist: bees and bee-keeping

Entomology: insects

Herpetology: amphibians and reptiles

Ichthyology: fish

Ornithology: birds

Zoology: animals, in general

Related to Species Survival

adapt: adjust to environmental conditions

adaptation: a physical or behavioral change that enables an organism to better adapt to changes in its environment

extinction: the loss of an entire species

Unicellular Organisms

unicellular: an organism made up of only one cell

amoeboid movement: use of pseudopods to move

flagella: long, whip-like structure that some unicellular organisms use for locomotion

pseudopod: a "false foot" membrane surrounded by cytoplasm extended from amoeba and used for locomotion

How an Organism Changes as it Matures

growth: an increase in size due to producing new cells

development: changes in the form of an organism as it proceeds to maturity

metamorphosis: changes in form as an organism matures; may be complete or incomplete

Miscellaneous Words to Know

photosynthesis: process by which green plants use energy form the sun to make food

stimulus: anything that causes a reaction by a living thing

homeostasis: maintaining a stable internal environment such as constant temperature or rate of respiration

Lesson 3: Outline

Characteristics of Life

I.   All living things are made with one or more cells.

    A. _____

    B. _____

    C. _____

II.   All living things must be able to obtain and use energy.

    A. _____

    B. _____

    C. _____

III.   All living things react to a stimulus.

    A. _____

    B. _____

    C. _____

IV.   All living things reproduce.

    A. _____

    B. _____

    C. _____

V.   All living things grow, develop, and die.

    A. _____

    B. _____

    C. _____

VI.   All living things maintain homeostasis.

    A. _____

    B. _____

    C. _____

1. What is biology?

2. What is a cell?

3. Which of the following sentences about cells are true?
    a. A cell is the smallest unit of an organism that can be considered alive.
    b. A multicellular organism may contain trillions of cells.
    c. A living thing that consists of a single cell is a multicellular organism.
    d. Organisms are made up of cells.

4. What are 2 types of reproduction?

5. Why does an organism need energy and a constant supply of materials?

6. What is metabolism?

7. What is homeostasis?

Evidence – factual information

Observations – information collected by using one or more of the senses

Data – the information that is gathered through observations

Quantitative data -

Qualitative data –information that is not easily quantified but is observed with senses

Inference – a logical interpretation of data based on one's prior knowledge and experience

Hypothesis – a possible explanation for a set of observations or an answer to a scientific problem based on prior knowledge, logical inferences, or imaginative guesses

Controlled experiment – a method of testing a hypothesis that utilizes a control group and an experimental group with only one variable (difference) between the control and experimental groups

Variable – one factor in an experiment that is 'manipulated' or changed from the control group

Independent (manipulating) variable –

Dependent (responding) variable – the observable or measurable results

Theory – a well-tested explanation that unifies a broad range of observations

Constant –

Experimental group – the manipulated group to which the independent variable is applied

Control group –

Scientific laws - must be simple, true, and universal. They are accepted at face value based upon the fact that they have always been observed to be true (note: there have been things accepted as "law" that were then shown to be false)

Metric System – a decimal system of measurement whose units are based on multiples of 10. Also shown as "SI" or International System of Measurement.

Tools for seeing small objects and organisms:

Microscopes – devices that produce magnified images of structures that are too small to see with the unaided eye

Light microscopes – produce magnified images by focusing visible light rays

Electron microscopes – powerful microscopes that use electromagnets to focus beams of electrons to visualize extremely small non-living objects

---

Spontaneous generation – the idea that life could arise from non-living things

Biogenesis –

Francesco Redi (Arezzo, February 18, 1626-Pisa, March 1, 1697) was an Italian physician. He is famous for his experiments, which tested the idea of "spontaneous generation." At the time, prevailing wisdom was that maggots formed magically from rotting meat.

What was his experiment?

Density – the mass per unit volume of an object; specific property of matter that can be used to identify different materials.

Technology – the use of scientific knowledge to improve the condition of mankind

Lesson 22: Cells and Homeostasis Terms

Types of Organisms

Unicellular organism – An organism having only one cell but carrying out all life functions

Multicellular – An organism with many cells, each of which is specialized to carry out various life functions

Eukaryotic cells –

Prokaryotic cells –

Cellular Energy

Energy – the ability to do work and/or maintain life in an organism

Photosynthesis –

Adenosine triphosphate (ATP) – the major source of readily available energy in cells; produced in the mitochondria when sugar and oxygen are chemically combined; energy released is transferred to a chemical known as ADP to make ATP

Change

Adaptation –

Mutation – any change in the genetic code that results in a physical or behavioral change

Parts of a Cell

Organelle –

Cell membrane – Outer layer of the cell that helps control what comes into and what goes out of the cell; AKA plasma membrane

Cell wall –

Centrioles – Cytoplasmic structures in animal cells that play a role in cell division by aiding spindle formation

Chloroplasts – Organelles in plant and algae cells that contain the green pigment chlorophyll that captures the suns energy; the place where plants make sugar

Chlorophyll –

Chromatin – made up of the tangled, threadlike, coils of chromosomes; contains DNA plus certain proteins

Chromosomes – worm-shaped structures that "condense" from chromatin before cells divide; contain DNA and protein; human body cells have two full sets of 23 different chromosomes

Cytoplasm – All the protoplasm located outside the nucleus but within the cell membrane

Deoxyribonucleic acid (DNA) – A long chemical shaped like a twisted ladder where the plans for running and reproducing cells are chemically stored; found mostly in the nucleus but small amounts have also been found in the mitochondria and chloroplasts

Endoplasmic reticulum – A network of tubular passageways surrounding the nuclear membrane used in transporting proteins; called "ER" and may be rough due to having ribosomes attached or be smooth; smooth ER also makes some lipids

Golgi complex – Made up of stacks of membranes that help process, package and deliver proteins from the endoplasmic reticulum

Lysosomes – Organelles rarely found in plants that contain digestive enzymes which break down food and digest worn out cell parts

Mitochondria (singular: mitochondrion) –

Nuclear – Refers to the cell nucleus

Food vacuole – A small sac created when the cell membrane surrounds a food particle

Nucleus (plural: nuclei) –

Nucleolus – "Little Nucleus;" the area of the nucleus where ribosomes are made; cells can have more than one nucleolus

Organelles – "Little Organs;" certain structures in the cytoplasm where specific tasks are carried out

Selectively permeable membrane – a membrane that only allows certain substances to pass through

Ribosome –

Vacuole – A large sac in plant cells that contains liquid

How Substances Move In and Out of Cells

Passive transport – the movement of substances across the plasma membrane without the use of the cell's energy

Diffusion –

Osmosis – water across the plasma membrane from areas of high concentration of solute (the dissolved substance in the water) to areas of lower concentration (less of the dissolved substance in the water)

Facilitated transport – occurs when a carrier molecule (similar to a tunnel) in the plasma membrane allows a substance to pass through it moving from the higher to the lower concentration of the substance but uses no energy in the process

Carrier proteins – special proteins that form tunnel-like openings in cell membranes that make is easier for large molecules to diffuse

Active transport – transport requires the use of the cell's energy (ATP) and special carrier molecules to move substances across the plasma membrane

Receptor Mediated Transport – when substances bind to specialized molecules on the cell surface before being engulfed

Endocytosis – the process by which large particles are brought into the cell. Amoeba feed by endocytosis

Exocytosis – the process by which large particles leave the cell

Pinocytosis – cells surrounding and absorbing liquids

Isotonic – when the concentration of dissolved substances is the same on both sides of the membrane

Hypotonic – a solution surrounding a cell has a lower concentration of the dissolved substance than the cell itself

Hypertonic – a solution surrounding a cell has a higher concentration of the dissolved substance than the cell itself

Solute – the dissolved substance in a solution

Solvent – the dissolving substance in a solution

Miscellaneous Words to Know

Proteins –

Enzymes – Proteins that control the rates of chemical reactions in cells; digestive enzymes such as pepsin and trypsin are produced by specialized cells to break down food in the digestive tract

Genetic code –

Development – a process in which an organism goes through predictable stages as it matures

Homeostasis – refers to maintaining stable internal conditions such as heart rate or temperature

Amoeba –

Cell division – The process that results in two cells being formed from one cell

Lesson 34: Osmosis Questions

1. How is osmosis related to diffusion?

2. What are the two things needed for osmosis to take place?

3. What does the term semi permeable or selectively permeable mean?

4. Define the following terms:
   a) Hypertonic:

   b) Hypotonic:

   c) Isotonic:

5. If you were to dissolve some sugar in a liter of water and then place some of this solution into a dialysis bag; then place the bag into a beaker of distilled water, what would happen to the size and weight of the bag of sugar water?

6. Explain the mechanism of what happened to the bag using the terms, concerning osmosis, you have learned in this course.

7. Draw out the above procedure and then explain what you would have to do to reverse the process.

8. Why do saltwater fish die when placed in freshwater? Explain your answer using what you have learned about osmosis.

Lesson 38: Properties of Water and pH

The Water Molecule

1. Draw a picture of a water molecule showing oxygen and two hydrogens bonded together.

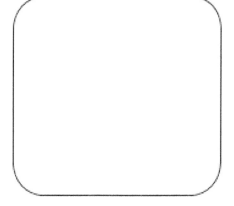

2. Why is a water molecule polar? Indicate the location of charges on the molecule you have drawn.

3. Is the following sentence true or false? A water molecule is neutral.

4. What causes water molecules to be attracted to each other?

5. Which of the following statements are true about hydrogen bonds?

   ❏ A hydrogen bond is stronger than an ionic bond.
   ❏ The attraction between the hydrogen atom on one water molecule and the oxygen atom on another water molecule is an example.
   ❏ A hydrogen bond is stronger than a covalent bond.
   ❏ They are the strongest bonds that form between molecules.

6. Distinguish between cohesion and adhesion.

7. Look at the picture of liquid in a glass tube (burette) at the right. What property of water is represented?

8. Why is capillary action important for plants?

9. What makes water a good solvent?

10. Sugar is dissolved in water to make a sugar solution.   What is the **solvent**? What is the **solute**?

11. Which type(s) of substances can water dissolve? (check all that apply)

    ❏ polar
    ❏ non-polar
    ❏ ionic
    ❏ hydrophilic
    ❏ hydrophobic

12. Why does ice float in liquid water?

13. How does the density of solid water help living organisms in lakes?

14. Water's high heat of vaporization makes it a good _____.

15. Why is water's high specific heat good for living things?

Acids, Bases, and pH

16. Water molecules can dissociate to form what two ions?

Lesson 38: Properties of Water and pH (cont.) Biology with Lab

17. Why is water neutral despite the production of hydrogen ions and hydroxide ions?

18. What does the pH scale indicate?

19. Complete the table to review pH:

Substance	pH range	amount of OH- and H+	Examples
Acid		more H+ than OH-	
Base			
Water	7		

20. How many more H + ions does a solution with a pH of 4 have than a solution with a pH of 5?

21. Why is a change in pH dangerous for cells?

22. What are buffers?

Lesson 41: Macromolecule Chart

	Carbohydrate	Lipid	Nucleic Acid	Protein
Organic? Y or N				
Composed of these elements				
Monomer(s)				
Functions/Uses in Living Things				
Examples				
Additional Information				

Lesson 45: Virtual Labs

Carbohydrates Lab:

1. List the steps and reagent used to test for simple sugars: what does a positive test reaction look like?

2. List the steps and reagent used to test for starch: what does a positive test reaction look like?

Protein Lab:

3. List the steps and reagent used to test for protein:

4. What does a positive test reaction look like?

Lipids Lab:

5. List the steps and reagent used to test for lipids:

6. What does a positive test reaction look like?

Foods:

Perform the carbohydrate, protein, and lipids tests on the foods shown and record the positive test results below:

Potatoes are a _____

Orange juice is a _____

Almonds _____

Eggs _____

Salmon _____

Milk _____

Converting stored chemical energy into usable ATP energy

Cellular respiration – the process of using oxygen in the mitochondria to chemically break down organic molecules such as glucose to release the energy stored in its bonds

Adenosine triphosphate (ATP) – from combining Adenosine diphosphate and phosphate; ATP is the main energy currency of cells.

Cellular respiration equation – $C_6H_{12}O_6 + 6O_2 \rightarrow 6CO_2 + 6H_2O$ (+ ATP ENERGY)

Glycolysis – a process in which one molecule of glucose is broken in half by enzymes in the cytoplasm, producing 2 molecules of pyruvic acid and only 2 molecules of ATP.

Aerobic respiration – all processes that require oxygen are described as "aerobic"

Fermentation – if sufficient oxygen is not present in the cell, glycolysis is followed by a different pathway called fermentation that produces very little energy and either alcohol or lactic acid depending on the organism

Anaerobic respiration – Processes that do not require oxygen are "anaerobic"

Mitochondria – organelle where cellular respiration occurs

Krebs cycle – also known as the Citric Acid Cycle, occurs in the mitochondrion after glycolysis and is the second of three phases of cellular respiration; it produces 2 ATP molecules, 10 energy carrier molecules, and CO_2 from each glucose molecule

Electron Transport Chain (ETC) – a series of chemical reactions that produces 34 ATP molecules and H2O from the carrier molecules that were produced in the Krebs cycle

Lactic acid fermentation – occurs in animal cells when there is no oxygen available; pyruvic acid is converted into a waste product called lactic acid

Alcoholic fermentation – occurs in some plants and unicellular organisms such as yeast and bacteria; the process converts pyruvic acid into ethyl alcohol and a carrier compound (giving off CO_2), which allows glycolysis to continue

Oxygen debt – occurs during anaerobic respiration because oxygen must be "paid back" to the cells to remove the lactic acid

Glucose – a six carbon sugar produced by photosynthesis

Heterotrophs (consumers) – organisms that cannot make their own food

Chemosynthesis – -process by which organisms use inorganic compounds as their energy supply

Photosynthesis

Photosynthesis equation – $6CO_2 + 6H_2O + (LIGHT\ ENERGY) \rightarrow C_6H_{12}O_6 + 6O_2$

Autotrophs (producers – use photosynthesis, to convert the energy in sunlight, carbon dioxide and water into chemical energy or food (glucose)

Visible spectrum – the resulting array of colors, ranging from red at one end to violet at the other; each color of light has different wavelengths, and a different amount of energy

Pigment – a molecule that absorbs certain wavelengths of light and reflects or transmits others

Chloroplast – organelle in plant cells where photosynthesis takes place

Chlorophyll *a* – directly involved in the light reactions of photosynthesis

Chlorophyll *b* – assists Chlorophyll a in capturing light energy

Accessory pigment – absorbs colors that chlorophyll a CANNOT absorb, the accessory pigments enable plants to capture more of the energy in light

Carotenoids – accessory pigments that include yellow, red, and orange pigments that color carrots, bananas, squash, flowers, and autumn leaves

Thylakoids – disk-shaped structures that contain photosynthetic pigments

Stroma – gel-like material that surrounds thylakoids

Grana – neatly folded layers of the thylakoids that resemble stacks of pancakes

Light dependent reactions – occur in the thylakoids; energy is captured from sunlight, water is split into hydrogen ions, electrons, and Oxygen (O_2). Photolysis is the splitting of a water molecule; light energy is converted to chemical energy, which is temporarily stored in ATP and NADPH. The electrons that absorbed the energy are passed along the electron transport chain (ETC) and store energy in ATP. NADP picks off the H^+ to form $NADPH^+$ and electrons from photolysis and stores it for later use.

Light independent reactions – occur in the stroma; a series of reactions referred to as the Calvin Cycle - the chemical energy stored in ATP and NADPH powers the formation of Organic Compounds (sugars), using carbon dioxide, CO_2 and the H^+ from the $NADPH^+$

Stromata – tiny holes underneath leaves where the exchange of gasses may occur from outside the leaf to inside the leaf

Photosynthesis – a complex series of chemical reactions that occurs in plants and some algae and bacteria whereby carbon dioxide and water are combined to form glucose and oxygen; the process requires the presence of both light and chlorophyll to occur

Energy

Endergonic chemical reaction – one in which free energy is required in order to proceed

Exergonic chemical reaction – one in which free energy is released

Energy – the ability to do work or cause change

Work – the ability to change or move matter against other forces

Lesson 52: Cellular Respiration Notes

The Flow of Energy

1. List some cellular tasks that require energy:

2. What is the source of all energy on Earth? _____

3. Which product of photosynthesis stores energy? _____

4. What form of chemical energy is useable by the cell? _____

5. Is energy recycled? _____

6. Write out the equation for Photosynthesis and Cell Respiration below:

Photosynthesis	
Cell Respiration	

7. Which of the above equations is catabolic? Which is anabolic? (Mark them with an A or C, respectively.)

8. Distinguish between autotrophs and heterotrophs. Which have chloroplasts? Which have mitochondria?

9. Draw the basic structure of ATP. Indicate on the drawing where you would break the bond to release energy. What molecule results when you break this bond? _____

10. List at least two other energy carrying molecules, other than ATP:

Aerobic Cellular Respiration

11. What is the purpose of cellular respiration?

12. How is cellular respiration different than burning fuel in a car? How is it the same?

13. Why is cellular respiration considered aerobic?

14. Label the mitochondrion with the following parts: **outer membrane, inner membrane (cristae), intermembrane space, matrix.**

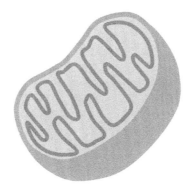

15. What does the word glycolysis mean?

16. Complete the Table below while reading about each stage of Cell Respiration:

Stage	Where it Occurs	What Goes In	What Comes Out
Glycolysis			
Krebs cycle			
Electron Transport Chain (ETC)			

Lesson 52: Cellular Respiration Notes (cont.) Biology with Lab

17. Can you add the missing pieces to this diagram after reading through the notes on the 3 stages of Cell Respiration?

    • Where is oxygen used?
    • Where is carbon dioxide released?

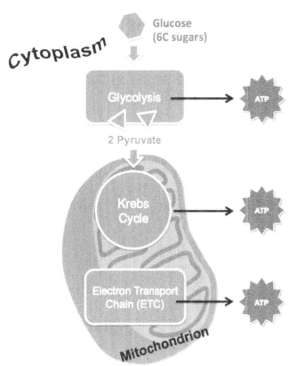

18. How many ATP are made during aerobic cellular respiration? _____

19. What role does ATP Synthase Play?

20. What is the purpose of oxygen in Cell Respiration?

21. Cellular respiration begins with a pathway called _____.

22. Is the following sentence True or False? Glycolysis releases a great amount of energy. _____

Name That Stage! Practice

23. Use this space to record the correct answers for this activity:

Glycolysis	Krebs Cycle	ETC

The Powerhouse of the Cell Movie

24. Distinguish between fast and slow twitch fibers. When are they used?
    Which have more mitochondria?

25. What does exercise training do for our muscle cells?

26. What damages mitochondrial DNA?

27. As a person ages, **what changes occur** that contributes to aging and lack
    of stamina?

Anerobic Respiration: Fermentation

28. Because fermentation does not require oxygen, it is said to be

    _____.

29. List the two main types of fermentation, distinguish between each using
    the table on the next page:

Fermentation Type	Where it Occurs	What Goes In	What Comes Out

How is each type of fermentation used commercially?

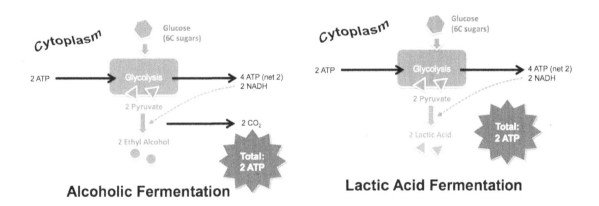

Alcoholic Fermentation   **Lactic Acid Fermentation**

30. During rapid exercise, how do your muscle cells produce ATP?

31. When a runner needs quick energy for a short race, what source can supply enough ATP for about 90 seconds?

32. Why does a sprinter have an oxygen debt to repay after the race is over?

Fermentation Separation Practice Activity

33. Make some notes about your learning from this activity:

Alcoholic Fermentation	Both	Lactic Acid Fermentation

Lesson 55: Photosynthesis Notes

Chloroplasts, Light and Pigments

1. Label the chloroplast with the following parts:
   outer membrane
   inner membrane
   thylakoid
   grana
   intermembrane space
   stroma.

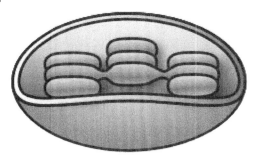

2. Chloroplasts contain saclike photosynthetic membranes called

   _____ where chlorophyll molecules are embedded. When

   stacked, these sac-like membranes make up _____.

3. White light is made up of which colors?

4. List the primary pigment in plants.

5. What is an accessory pigment? Give at least two examples of accessory pigments.

6. Both chlorophyll a and b absorb _____ and _____ light, but

   both reflect _____ light.

Photosynthesis

7. Write the overall equation for photosynthesis using words.

8. Write the overall equation for photosynthesis using chemical formulas.

9. Photosynthesis uses the energy of sunlight to convert water and

   carbon dioxide into oxygen and high-energy _____.

10. What are the two stages of photosynthesis called?
    a.
    b.

11. Complete the following table:

Stage	Where It Occurs	What Goes In	What Comes Out
Light dependent reactions			
Light Independent Reactions (Calvin Cycle)			

Light Dependent Reactions

Make notes about the Light Reactions on this diagram as necessary.

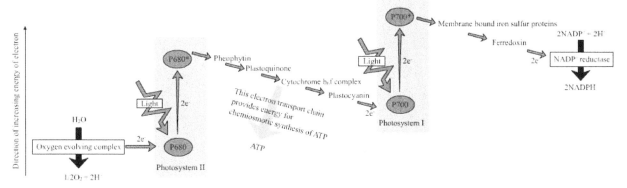

"Z-scheme" by w:User:Bensaccount: http://en.wikipedia.org/wiki/Image:Z-scheme.png. Licensed under Creative Commons Attribution - Share Alike 3.0 via Wikimedia Commons - http://commons.wikimedia.org/wiki/File:Z-scheme.png#mediaviewer/File:Z-scheme.png

12. Complete the following summary of the Light Reactions using the word bank:

ATP   electron   NADPH   oxygen   photolysis

When light hits the photosystems, it jars loose an _____,

which becomes energized and then enters an Electron Transport Chain.

The Electron Transport Chains are used to generate _____ and

_____, energy carrier molecules. Photosystem II's

missing electron is replaced by the splitting of water, also called

_____, which gives off _____ gas as a by-product.

The oxygen we breathe originates from the _____ that plants

use in photosynthesis.

Light Independent Reactions (Calvin Cycle)
Make notes about the Calvin cycle on this diagram as necessary.

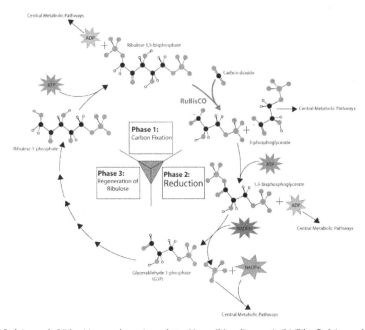

"Calvin-cycle2" by User: adenosine - http://en.wikipedia.org/wiki/File:Calvin-cycle2.png#mediaviewer/File:Calvin-cycle2.png Licensed under Creative Commons Attribution-Share Alike 2.5

13. True or False: The light independent reactions happen during the dark only.

14. What does it mean to "fix" carbon in the Calvin Cycle?

15. How many turns of the Calvin Cycle make a single molecule of glucose?

16. The Calvin Cycle uses ATP and NADPH energy to build the sugar glucose. Where did it get the ATP and NADPH?

Lesson 55: Photosynthesis Notes (cont.)

17. What are three factors that affect the rate at which photosynthesis occurs?
    a.
    b.
    c.

18. For each graph below, describe the reasons that the rate of photosynthesis changes:

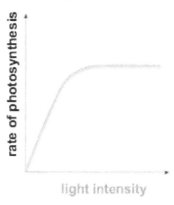
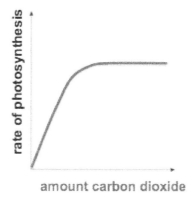
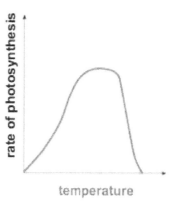

19. Is the following sentence true or false? Increasing the intensity of light decreases the rate of photosynthesis.

20. What are stomata, and how do they help a plant with photosynthesis?

Cellular Respiration

$C_6H_{12}O_6$	+	$6O_2$	$\rightarrow$	$6CO_2$	+	$6H_2O$	+	Energy
(Molecule name)		(Molecule name)		(Molecule name)		(Molecule name)		
and		and	form	and		and		36 ATP
Cut out one $C_6H_{12}O_6$ molecule and glue here		Cut out six O_2 molecules and glue here		Cut out six CO_2 molecules and glue here		Cut out six H_2O molecules and glue here		

Circle the pictures below of the organisms that undergo Cellular Respiration.

Photosynthesis

6CO₂	+	6H₂O	+	Light	→	C₆H₁₂O₆	+	6O₂
(Molecule name)		(Molecule name)				(Molecule name)		(Molecule name)
and		and		and energy	form	and		
Cut out six CO₂ molecules and glue here		Cut out six H₂O molecules and glue here				Cut out one C₆H₁₂O₆ molecule and glue here		Cut out six O₂ molecules and glue here

Circle the pictures below of the organisms that undergo Photosynthesis.

(This page left intentionally blank)

Lesson 58: Cut Outs

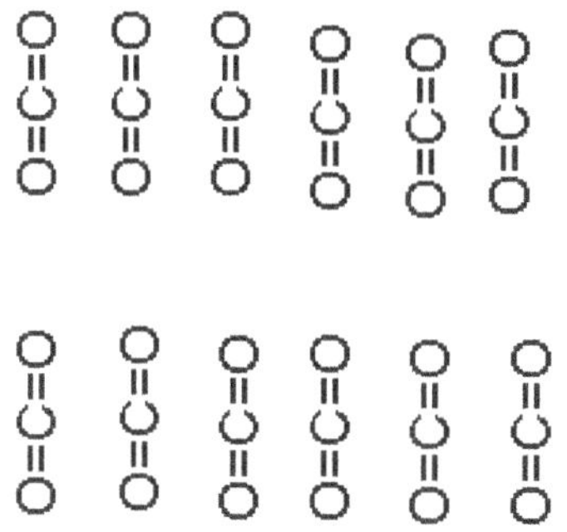

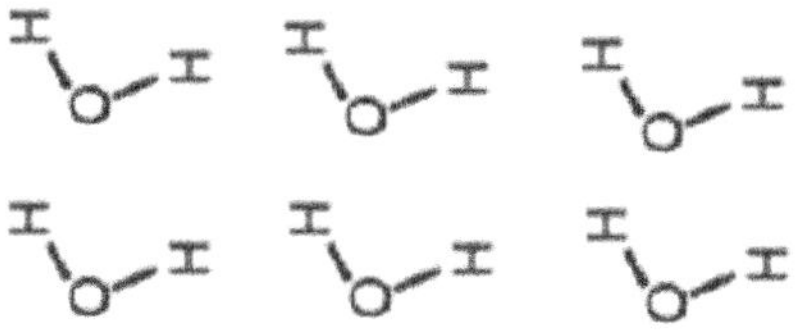

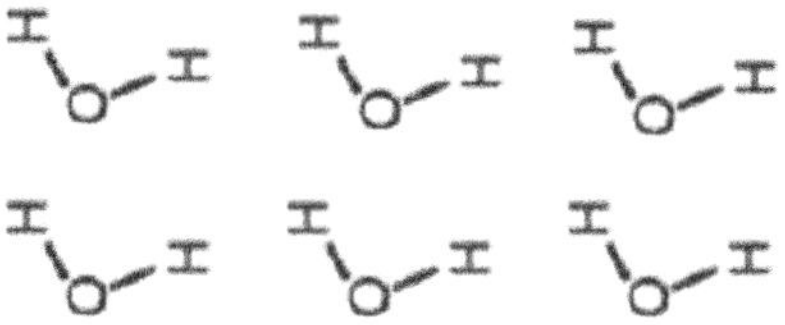

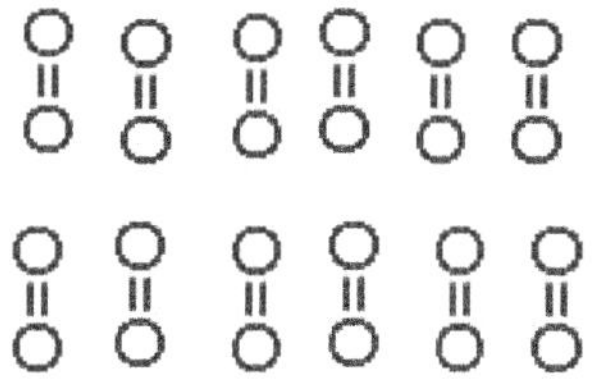

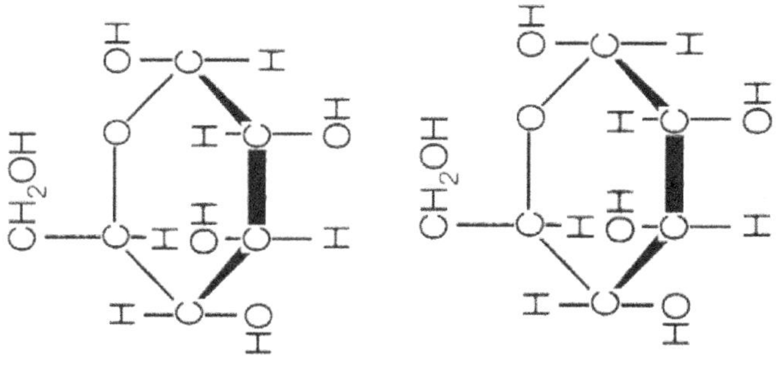

(This page left intentionally blank)

Chemical Energy and Food

1. Cellular respiration begins with a pathway called _____.

2. True or false: Glycolysis produces less energy than aerobic respiration.

Overview of Cellular Respiration

3. Explain cellular respiration in your own words.

4. What is the equation for cellular respiration using chemical formulas?

Fermentation

5. What is fermentation?

6. Because fermentation does not require oxygen, it is said to be _____.

7. What are the two main types of fermentation?

    1.

    2.

8. Explain the process of alcoholic fermentation.

9. During rapid exercise, how do your muscle cells produce ATP?

Energy and Exercise

10. When a runner needs quick energy for a short race, what source can supply enough ATP for about 90 seconds?

11. Why does a sprinter have an oxygen debt to repay after the race is over?

Comparing Photosynthesis and Cellular Respiration

12. If photosynthesis is the process that deposits energy in a savings account, then what is cellular respiration?

13. How are photosynthesis and cellular respiration opposite in terms of carbon dioxide?

14. How are photosynthesis and cellular respiration opposite in terms of oxygen?

Lesson 65: Cell Reproduction Terms

1. **Cell division** – the organized process of creating two new cells; consists of both mitosis and meiosis followed by cytokinesis.

2. **Cell cycle** – timeline of events that occurs during the lifetime of a cell; involves both interphase and cell division.

3. **Mitosis** – when the nucleus of a cell divides into two identical nuclei.

4. **Cytokinesis** – when the rest of the cell divides to form two daughter cells.

5. **Chromatin** – form of DNA inside the nucleus that appears as disorganized, long strands.

6. **Chromosomes** – form of tightly coiled, shortened and thickened DNA; appears prior to DNA replication and therefore mitosis; can refer to a duplicated chromosome or a sister chromatid that has been separated from its partner sister chromatid.

7. **Sister chromatids** – the two sides of the "X" formed by replicated chromosomes; connected by centromere; together they can be called a duplicated chromosome.

8. **Centromere** – a central protein bundle that connects sister chromatids.

9. **Karyotype** – a picture of the chromosomes within an organism's body cells, arranged by homologous pairs; used as a way to determine sex and diagnose some disorders.

10. **Autosomes** – all chromosomes except for the sex chromosomes.

11. **Sex chromosomes** – in many species such as humans, the chromosomes received from parents determine the sex of a child; the human's 23rd chromosome pair determines whether the child is a male (XY) or female (XX).

12. **Homologous pairs** – matching chromosomes that each came from one parent (father, mother); homologs code for different versions of the same genes.

13. **Gene** – a length of DNA that codes for a protein/trait.

14. **Alleles** – two alternate forms of each gene present on a specific chromosome in an organism (such as blue or brown eyes); with two copies of each chromosome, you have two alleles for each gene.

15. **Tumor** – an abnormal mass of tissue caused by excessive cell growth.

16. **Mutation** – a change in the DNA code of an organism.

Lesson 65: Cell Reproduction Terms (cont.)

17. **Spindle fibers** – thin protein filaments that are constructed by the centrioles in prophase; during cell division (mitosis or meiosis) they assist in guiding the chromosomes to separate properly.

18. **Cell plate** – a structure which eventually forms a cell wall between daughter cells during cytokinesis; occurs in plants or other organisms with a cell wall.

19. **Cleavage furrow** – the indentation or pinched area of the cell surface that begins cytokinesis; not seen in organisms with a cell wall.

20. **Meiosis** – the division of a nucleus that results in four nuclei with one half the original number of chromosomes; used to produce gametes.

21. **Diploid number** – the total number of chromosomes in normal body cells; two matching homologs of each kind.

22. **Haploid number** – one half the total number of chromosomes in a normal body cell; one of each kind of homolog.

23. **Tetrad** – homologous chromosomes from each parent pair up to form two attached sets of chromatids ("tetra" = four for the four chromatids).

24. **Crossing over** – each chromatid may exchange a part of itself with its homolog as it crosses over the other during late prophase 1 or early metaphase 1 of meiosis.

25. **Genetic recombinations** – different ways chromosomes can provide variation in the species depending on which chromosomes are inherited and whether or not crossing over occurs.

26. **Gametogenesis** – production of gametes by meiosis; oogenesis and spermatogenesis are the two types.

27. **Oogenesis** – meiosis that produces eggs (ova).

28. **Ovum** – haploid, female reproductive cell; also called an egg.

29. **Spermatogenesis** – meiosis that produces sperm.

30. **Sperm** – haploid, male reproductive sex cell.

31. **Somatic cell** – body cell (liver, skin, stomach, etc.).

32. **Gametes** – sex cells; sperm and egg cells.

Lesson 66: The Cell Cycle

Stage of the Cell Cycle	Events of the Stage	Part of Cell Division? Y or N
Interphase: G1 (also GO)		
Interphase: S		
Interphase: G2		
M: Mitosis		
Cytokinesis		

Overview: In this activity, you will examine a photograph of cells from the growing tip of an onion root and predict the duration of each stage of mitosis.

Not all of the root cells are dividing, as the image below shows you; only the region of the root called the **apical meristem** will have cells that are actively dividing using mitosis. Take a look at a slice of this region of the onion root:

Apical meristem
the location of root growth, or mitosis

You will not be completing a full lab report, but rather a hypothesis, table, and answers to thought-provoking discussion questions. The rubric for grading is on the last page of this lesson's packet.

Goal: Predict the length of time that onion cells spend in each phase of the cell cycle.

Hypothesis: Think about your learning on mitosis and the cell cycle so far. Make a prediction about how many minutes/hours each phase lasts:
- Interphase
- Prophase
- Metaphase
- Anaphase
- Telophase

Directions:
Collect Data: Examine the photograph on the following page.

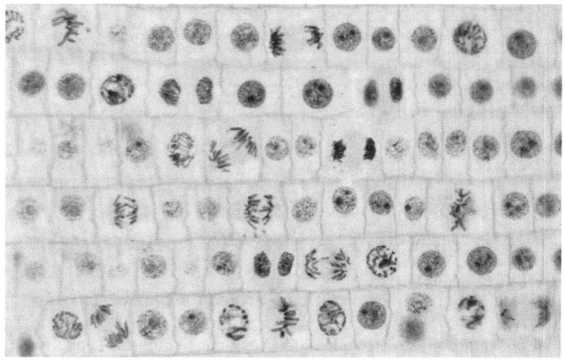

For each of the cells pictured, decide its phase. Keep a tally of how many are in each phase; record the total in the first row of the table on the next page. Sometimes it is most helpful to work in rows of cells so that you can keep track of where you leave off. If there is not a nucleus visible, do not include that cell in the count.

Calculate:

1. Record your number of cells in each stage in the first row of the table. Be sure your total cells counted was between 50 and 60.

2. For each phase, divide the number of cells in that phase by the total number of cells counted. Record this as a percent in the second row and check that this row adds up to 100%.
   Example: You counted 15 metaphase cells out of 60. 15/60 = 0.25 (25%)

3. Hours Spent in Each Phase: Multiply your *decimal* percent by 24 hours. Record this in the third row. Check that this row adds up to 24 hours.
   Example: 25% of your cells were in metaphase. 0.25 x 24 = 6 hours

	Interphase	Prophase	Metaphase	Anaphase	Telophase	Total
Number of Cells in each stage						**(50-60):**
Percent (%) of cells in each stage						**100%**
Hours spent in each stage						**24 hours**

Discussion Questions:

Answer each question in thoughtful, detailed and complete sentences.

1. What phase are most cells found in? Was your hypothesis supported?

2. Which phase takes the longest to complete? Explain why this makes sense.

3. Which phase is the shortest in length? Explain why this makes sense.

4. Some drugs used to fight cancer interfere with spindle fibers doing their job. Describe how this would stop cancer cells from increasing in number.

5. How does mitosis help an organism to grow in size?

Lesson 71: Mitosis Timeline Lab Rubric

Grading Rubric:

The following criteria should be used to evaluate your lab:

Criteria	Points Possible
Introduction State Hypothesis only • If-then statement • Includes prediction for each phase • Testable • Full sentence, proper spelling/grammar	5
Results Data Table • Properly set up per example • Accurate data for counted phases (row 1) • Each calculation is done properly (row 2,3)	20
Discussion Questions • 5 points per question • Answered in complete sentences	25
TOTAL	**50**

Lesson 72: Mitosis and Cytokinesis Questions   Biology with Lab

1. Is the following sentence true or false? Chromosomes are visible in most cells except during cell division.

2. At the beginning of cell division, what does each chromosome consist of?

3. _____ is the area where each pair of chromatids is attached.

4. The period of growth in between cell divisions is called _____.

5. Write the names of each of the four phases of the cell cycle:

    Cell growth =

    DNA replication =

    Preparation for mitosis =

    Mitosis and Cytokinesis =

6. The division of the nucleus during the M phase of the cell cycle is called

    _____.

7. What happens during the G1 phase?

8. What happens during the S phase?

9. What happens during the G2 phase?

10. What is the name for the two tiny structures located in the cytoplasm near the nuclear envelope at the beginning of prophase?

    a. centrioles   b. spindles   c. centromeres   d. chromatids

11. What is the spindle?

For questions 12-17, match the description of the event with the phase of mitosis it is in. Each phase may be used more than once.

    A. Prophase   B. Metaphase   C. Anaphase   D. Telophase

12. _____The chromosomes move until they form two groups near the poles of the spindle.

13. _____The chromosomes become visible.

14. _____A nuclear envelope re-forms around each cluster of chromosomes.

15. _____The centrioles take up positions on opposite sides of the nucleus.

16. _____The chromosomes line up across the center of the cell.

17. _____The nucleolus becomes visible in each daughter nucleus.

18-21: Label each phase.

22. What is cytokinesis?

23. How does cytokinesis occur in most animal cells?

24. What forms midway between the divided nucleus during cytokinesis in plant cells?

    a. cell nucleus   b. cytoplasm   c. cell plate   d. cytoplasmic organelles

1. What does it mean when two sets of chromosomes are homologous?

2. Which of these describes a diploid cell?

   a. 2N

   b. Contains two sets of homologous chromosomes

   c. Contains a single set of homologous chromosomes

   d. A gamete

3. If a *Drosophila* cell has a diploid number of 8, what is its haploid number?

   a. 8   b. 4   c. 2   d. 0

Phases of Meiosis

4. Why is meiosis described as a process of reduction division?

5. What are the two distinct stages of meiosis?

6. True or false: The diploid cell that enters meiosis becomes 4 haploid cells at the end of meiosis?

7. How does a tetrad form in prophase I of meiosis?

8. What is the number of chromatids in a tetrad?

   a. 8   b. 6   c. 4   d. 2

9. What is the result of the process of crossing-over during prophase I?

10. Circle the letter for **each** sentence that is true about meiosis.

   a. During meiosis I, homologous chromosomes separate.

   b. The two daughter cells produced by meiosis I still have the two complete sets of chromosomes as a diploid cell does.

   c. During anaphase II, the paired chromatids separate.

   d. After meiosis II, the four daughter cells contain the diploid number of chromosomes.

Gamete Formation

Match the products of meiosis with the descriptions.

eggs   sperm   polar bodies

11. Haploid gametes produced in males _____

12. Haploid gametes produced in females _____

13. Cells produced in females that do not participate in reproduction

   _____

14. Circle the letter for **each** sentence that is true about mitosis and meiosis.

   a. Mitosis produces four genetically different haploid cells.

   b. Meiosis produces two genetically identical diploid cells.

   c. Mitosis begins with a diploid cell.

   d. Meiosis begins with a diploid cell.

Double helix – the shape of the DNA molecule; consists of two nucleotide chains that wrap around each other to form a double spiral

Nucleotides – the monomers that make up DNA and RNA; consists of a nitrogen base (A, C, T, U, or G), a sugar, and a phosphate molecule

Adenine (A) – nitrogenous base found in DNA and RNA; pairs with T or U

Guanine (G) – nitrogenous base found in DNA and RNA; pairs with C

Cytosine (C) – nitrogenous base found in DNA and RNA; pairs with G

Thymine (T) – nitrogenous base found in DNA only; pairs with A

Uracil (U) – nitrogenous base found in RNA only; pairs with A

Purines – nitrogenous bases that have a double ring of carbon and nitrogen atoms; Adenine and Guanine

Pyrimidines – nitrogenous bases that have a single ring of carbon and nitrogen atoms; Cytosine, Thymine, and Uracil

Complementary – matching, as in complementary bases: A matches T or U; C matches G

Semi-conservative replication – specific type of replication in DNA that results in two double-stranded DNA molecules; each new molecule has half the original strand and have that is a complimentary (newly built) strand

Hydrogen bonds – weak attractions between molecules; hydrogen bonds hold the rungs of the DNA ladder together, but can be easily broken and reformed

Helicase – enzyme that unwinds and unzips DNA

Ligase – enzyme that creates bonds between sugars and phosphates in a growing DNA or RNA strand as it is being built

DNA Polymerase – enzymes that can bind to a single (unwound and separated) DNA strand, read it, and synthesize a new strand of complementary DNA; some are able to proofread their work

Protein synthesis – the formation of proteins using information coded on DNA and carried out by RNA in the ribosome

Messenger RNA (or mRNA) – a single uncoiled strand of RNA that transmits information from DNA to the ribosomes during protein synthesis

Transfer RNA (or tRNA) – a single folded strand of RNA that bonds with and carries a specific amino acid

Ribosomal RNA (or rRNA) – a globular form of RNA that is the major constituent of the ribosomes

Transcription – the process of forming a mRNA strand from a DNA strand in the nucleus

RNA polymerase – enzyme used in protein synthesis (translation) to read a DNA gene and compose a complementary mRNA strand

Codon – a 3-nucleotide mRNA sequence that codes for one specific amino acid

Start codon – specific coding sequence where mRNA transcription begins

Stop codon – a coding sequence signaling the end of the gene to be transcribed

Translation – the formation of proteins in the cytoplasm using information coded on mRNA and carried out by the ribosome

Anticodon – one end of a tRNA molecule that contains a set of three nucleotides that will compliment codons on the mRNA during translation; has a site for a specific amino acid on the opposite end

Mutation – any change in the DNA's letter (nitrogenous base) sequence

Point mutation – a change in a single nitrogen base in DNA; may or may not cause a change in the amino acid depending on position of letter changed

Frameshift mutation – the addition or deletion of a nitrogen base, causing a shift in codons so that the gene sequence is nonsense

Mutagen – anything that causes a mutation

Human Genome Project – an international effort to determine all the base pairs of the human genome

DNA fingerprinting – Scientists utilize the genetic "fingerprints" where DNA is broken into pieces and examined for patterns

Gene therapy – treats a genetic disorder by introducing a gene into a cell or by correcting a defect in a cell's genome

Genetic engineering – used to identify genes for specific traits or to transfer genes from one organism to another organism; involves the making of recombinant DNA in a lab

Recombinant DNA – a combination of DNA from two or more sources

Genetically Modified Organisms (GMOs) – any organism whose DNA has been modified by genetic engineering

Cloning – refers to any of a number of biotechnologies that aim to reproduce a genetic copy of an entire organism

Lesson 79: The Structure of DNA Notes Biology with Lab

1. The two strands of DNA intertwine to form a shape known as a

   _____.

2. What two things make up the backbone, or sides of DNA?

3. Where are the bases located in the DNA molecule?

4. DNA has an overall **positive/negative** charge (circle one). What is the cause of this?

5. **Pyrimidine** bases are composed of _____ ring(s).

6. **Purine** bases are composed of _____ ring(s).

7. What contributes to the stability of the DNA molecule?

8. Draw a line to below to match up the bases that pair up across the strand of DNA:

Adenine (A)	**Guanine (G)**
Cytosine (C)	**Thymine (T)**

9. What type of bonds connect these base pairs?

10. What does '**complimentary**' base pairing mean?

Lesson 83: DNA Workshop Questions

1. What is DNA replication?

2. In a real cell, the molecule unwinds from spools made of _____.

3. What helps unzip the DNA ladder?

4. What is the base pair rule?

5. How many bases are in the DNA chain?

6. What is the base sequence from top to bottom of the molecule on the right?

7. What is the base sequence from top to bottom of the molecule on the left?

8. Are the two sequences identical?

9. How many base pairs does each human chromosome contain?

10. All 46 chromosomes contain _____ pairs.

11. Where are you in the cell during DNA replication? Nucleus or cytoplasm?

12. What happens during protein synthesis?

13. At this point, DNA resembles a _____.

14. What moves up the ladder breaking the rungs?

15. What is the base pair rule for RNA?

16. What is the base sequence from the top to the bottom of the molecule?

17. Which side is the RNA molecule? How do you know?

18. In a real cell, how long would the RNA molecule be?

19. An RNA molecule transcribed from DNA is called _____.

20. Where will the new RNA molecule go now?

21. Where are you in the cell now?

22. What is the function of ribosomes?

23. What is a codon?

24. What is an anticodon?

25. What is attached to the tRNA molecule?

26. What is the first amino acid in this sequence?

Lesson 83: DNA Workshop Questions (cont.) Biology with Lab

27. What is the first codon sequence and its compliment?

28. What is the second codon sequence and its compliment (anticodon)?

29. What is the name of the second amino acid in this sequence?

30. Where will the ribosome go next?

31. What will happen to the first tRNA?

32. What is the third codon sequence and its compliment (anticodon)?

33. What is the name of the third amino acid in this sequence?

34. How long is the protein now?

35. How long can the protein chain get?

36. When will protein synthesis end?

37. What will the ribosome do when the end is reached?

38. What is the correct amino acid sequence of your protein that you just made?

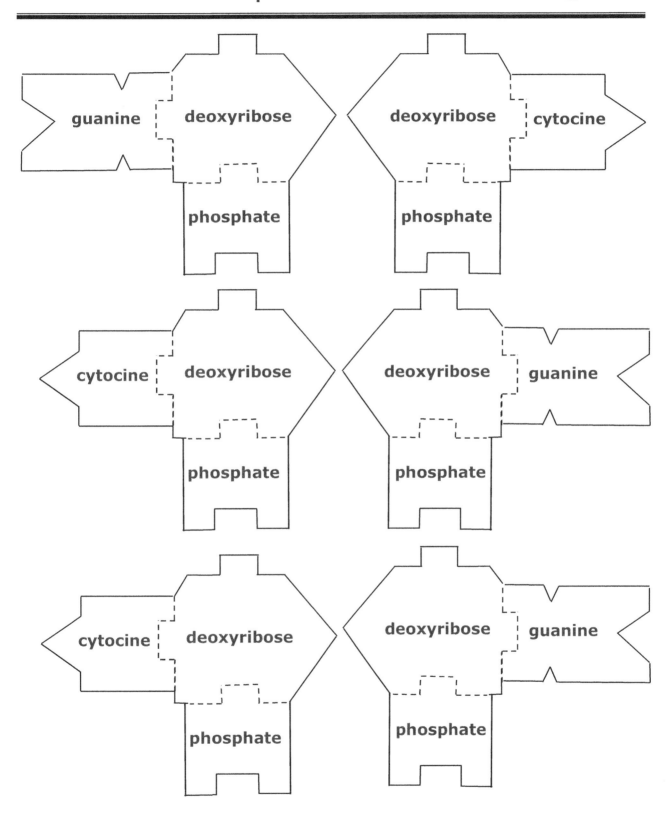

(This page left intentionally blank)

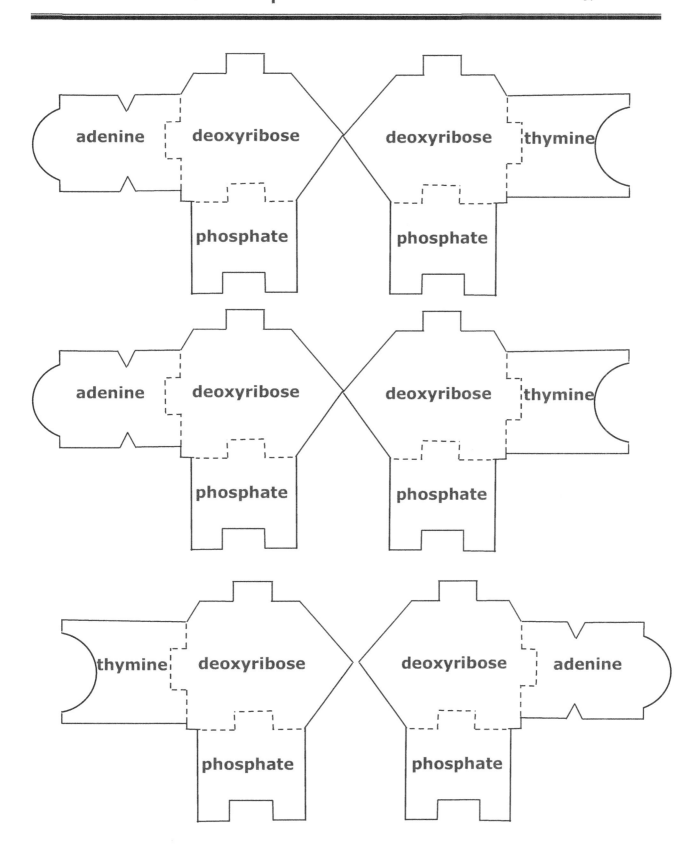

(This page left intentionally blank)

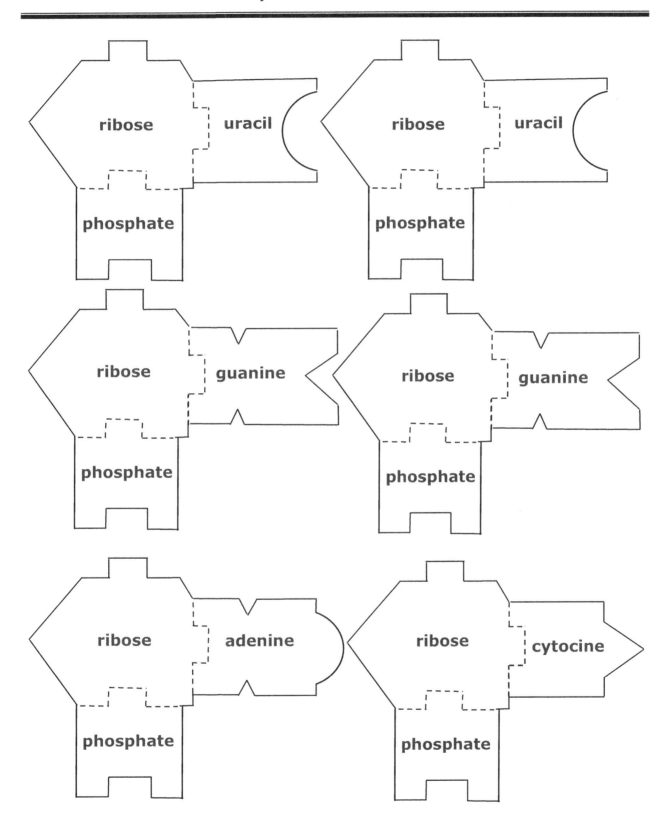

(This page left intentionally blank)

Lesson 91: Genetics Key Terms

Trait: a feature that an organism displays that is inherited

Genetics: the study of the traits of organisms

Heredity: passing traits from one generation to the next

Self-pollinated: plants whose pollen can normally pollinate only its own eggs

Cross pollinated: plants whose pollen is artificially transferred to another plant

Purebred (or true breeding): organisms that have alleles for one specific trait Gregor Mendel (known as the father of modern genetics

P generation (or parents): the two organisms whose genes produce offspring

F1 generation: the offspring from parents

F2 generation: the offspring produced by crossing two F1 individuals

Principle of Dominance and Recessiveness: one factor in a pair may mask the effect of the other

Principle of Segregation: the two factors for a characteristic separate during the formation of eggs and sperm

Principle of Independent Assortment: the factors for different characteristics are distributed to reproductive cells independently

Probability: the likely outcome a given event will occur from random chance

Phenotype: the external appearance of an organism; refers to the physical appearance of the individual

Genotype: the genetic makeup of an organism; refers to the alleles an individual receives at fertilization

Homozygous dominant: genotypes possess two dominant alleles for a trait (TT)

Homozygous recessive: genotypes possess two recessive alleles for a trait (tt)

Heterozygous: genotypes possess one of each allele for a particular trait (Tt); the allele not expressed in a heterozygote is a recessive allele

Punnett Square: a chart drawn to determine the probable results of a genetic cross

Monohybrid cross: a cross between individuals with one pair of contrasting genes (i.e., height)

Dihybrid cross: a cross between individuals with two pairs of contrasting genes (i.e., height and color)

Testcross: cross used to test if an organism is homozygous dominant (ex: AA) or heterozygous dominant (Aa); unknown (A?) is crossed with a known homozygous recessive (aa) to determine its genotype

Complete dominance: a pattern of inheritance where heterozygous offspring display dominant phenotype

Incomplete dominance: a pattern of inheritance where heterozygous offspring show trait intermediate between two parental phenotypes

Lethal alleles: a genetic defect that causes 100% mortality in the offspring

Co-dominance: a pattern of inheritance in which both alleles of a gene are expressed in a heterozygote

Sex-linked traits: have genes located on a sex chromosome (X or Y in humans)

Sex-linked inheritance: because the gene in question is on a sex chromosome, both sexes do not show the same probability for inheritance of a trait; for example: X-linked traits would show two alleles for females (X^aX^a) whereas males only have one allele (X^aY) that is expressed as a phenotype

Multiple-allele traits: controlled by three or more alleles of the same gene

Polygenic traits: controlled by two or more genes

Pleiotropy: one gene results in multiple (seemingly unrelated) phenotypes

Sex-influenced traits: located on autosomes but express themselves differently in the sexes because of sex hormones

Pedigree: graphic method of illustrating inheritance of genetic traits within several generations of families

Carrier: an individual that does not express, but carries the trait/allele for a phenotype (usually a disorder)

Sex-linked disorders: mutations of a chromosome located on a sex chromosome; disorder occurs more frequently in males since they have only one X and if it is defective, the individual expresses the disorder; females would need two defective X chromosomes to express the disorder (i.e., color blindness, Duchenne's Muscular Dystrophy, hemophilia)

Co-dominant disorder: a single dominant allele will cause some phenotypic disorder, but not the life-threatening condition (i.e., sickle cell anemia)

Dominant allele disorders: genetic mutations in a dominant allele; a single dominant allele causes the disorder (i.e., Huntington's Disease and Achondroplasia)

Recessive Allele Disorders: genetic mutations in recessive alleles; two recessive alleles are required to express the disorder

Chromosomal disorders: mutations in which an entire chromosome pair fails to separate properly in meiosis; results in one or three of the homolog; (i.e., Turner Syndrome, Down Syndrome, Klinefelter's Syndrome)

Lesson 99: Reebop Lab

Overview: Reebops (*Marshmella magicus*) are an imaginary species that reproduce at a rapid rate. In this activity, you will assume the role of two Reebop parents reproducing to make an offspring. You will simulate meiosis, fertilization, and then build your baby Reebop by decoding the alleles on the chromosomes. Some basic facts about Reebops:

- Reebops have 8 homologous chromosome pairs, each with one trait.
- The 8th chromosome is a sex chromosome. It determines the sex of the baby and carries the gene for eye type.

Goal: Mate two Reebops to create a baby Reebop. Record and analyze your data.

Lab Materials:

- Scissors
- Printed copies of the mom and dad chromosomes
- Blue and pink crayon
- Materials from your home (see Reebop Decoder Key)

Directions:

1. **Print and cut out the parent chromosomes from the last pages of this lab.**
   Using your blue and pink crayons, mark or color each strip for Dad blue and for Mom pink. You might do this before cutting so you don't lose track of which set is which.

2. **Create parents.**
   Match up homologous chromosomes (by length) for mom. Repeat for dad. Record the parent genotypes in *Data Table 1*. Use the *Reebop Decoder Key* to determine genotypes and record in *Data Table 1*. Use *Reebop Decoder Key* to build parent Reebops (you can do this with raw materials or create it digitally). Take pictures and place in *Data Table 1*.

3. Make a prediction.

What do you think your baby Reebop will look like? Look at the *Reebop Decoder Key* (page 5 of this lab) and your parent genotypes you have placed in *Data Table 1*. Do some Punnett Squares. Which genotypes/ phenotypes are most likely with these two parents? Write a hypothesis for the baby's genotype and phenotype in *Data Table 1* with an explanation.

4. Simulate meiosis for each parent.

- **Spermatogenesis:** Place all the father's (blue) chromosomes face down. Match them up by size. Select one chromosome of each size to make up a sperm with 8 chromosomes. *Note: the sex chromosomes will not match up.*

- **Oogenesis**: Using the mother's (pink) chromosomes, repeat the same process to create an egg.

- Set the unused chromosomes aside. You should now have two piles of chromosomes: 8 blue chromosomes (sperm) and 8 pink chromosomes (egg).

5. Simulate fertilization.

Combine your sperm and egg to make a Reebop baby.

6. Record data.

Turn over the chromosomes and record the following in Data Table 1:
- Your baby Reebop's name and sex
- Baby's genotype and phenotype (using the *Reebop Decoder Key*) for each trait

7. Build your baby.

Use the *Reebop Decoder Key* to build your baby Reebop (raw materials or digitally). Take a picture and place in *Data Table 1*.

8. Answer Discussion Questions.

Data Table 1. Reebop Mating Data

Reebop	Genotype	Phenotype	Picture of Reebop
Mom	*list all letters here* *Example:* *AABbccDd….*	*list phenotypes here* *2 Antenna …*	*insert picture here (built with household objects from Reebop Decoder Key or digitally drawn)*
Dad			
Prediction for Baby			**Explanation:** *(no picture needed)*
Baby's name: _____ Baby's Sex: _____			

Discussion Questions:

1. Compare your baby to his/her parents. Does s/he have the same genotype? Does s/he have the same phenotype? Why or why not?

2. Compare your prediction to the actual baby's genotype or phenotype. Chances are you were not 100% accurate. Explain why or why not.

3. The picture at the top of the lab is an older sibling of your baby! Which two laws from Mendel support the idea that siblings are not identical even though they come from the same parent?

4. Which traits in Reebops appear to "blend" and show incomplete dominance?

5. Which traits in Reebops appear to show complete dominance?

6. The parents in this cross actually have 12 other Reebop babies. Of them, 6 males and 1 female are blind. Why does a difference exist in the number of females with blindness than without blindness? *Hint: Use a Punnett Square to support your argument.*

Reebop Decoder Key
use toothpicks to connect body parts as necessary

Trait	Genotypes/Phenotypes	Suggested Materials to Use
Body Segments (does not include head)	DD or Dd = three segments dd = two segments	regular marshmallows
Humps	MM = 2 humps Mm = 1 hump mm = no humps	mini marshmallows
Legs	LL = four legs Ll = two legs ll = no legs	toothpicks
Tail	TT or Tt = curly tail tt = straight tail	paperclip
Nose	QQ = red Qq = green qq = yellow	Colored candy or objects (gumdrops/thumbtacks)
Antennae	AA = two antennae Aa = one antenna aa = no antennae	nails or screws
Eye Number	EE or Ee = 2 eyes ee = 3 eyes	pins or thumbtacks
Blindness	B, BB or Bb = sighted (eyes present) b or bb = blind (remove eyes)	n/a
Sex	XX = female XY = male	n/a

a m D q x A M d Q

T   B   t   E

   e   l

      L

         x

         b

(This page left intentionally blank)

Lesson 99: Reebop Lab - Dad

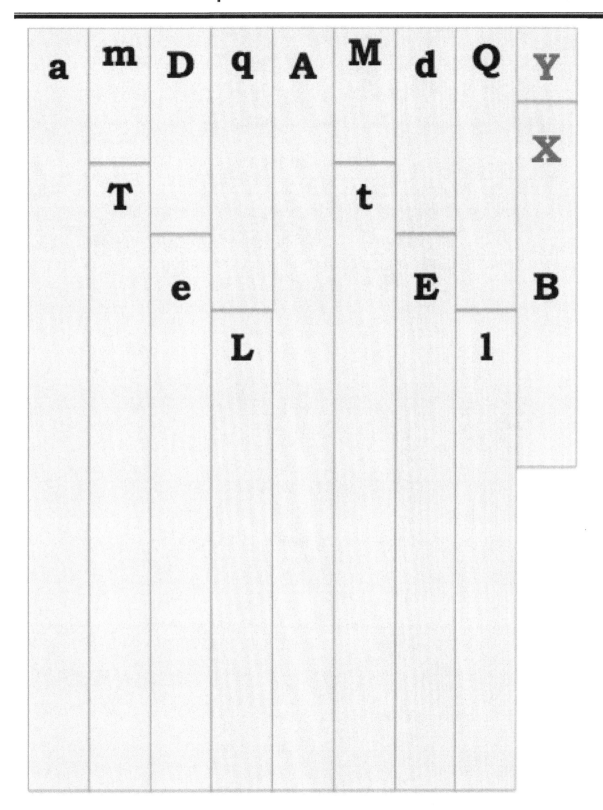

(This page left intentionally blank)

Lesson 105: Ecology Key Terms

Introduction to Ecology

Ecology: study of the interactions between organisms and the nonliving components of their environment

Biosphere: the portion of the Earth (air, water, and land) where living things exist

Biotic: living things that shape or affect an ecosystem

Abiotic: non-living things or factors that shape or affect an ecosystem

Ecosystem: all organisms and the nonliving environment in a defined area

Population: all the members of the same species that live in a defined area at one time

Organism: the simplest level of organization in ecology; a living thing

Biome: ecosystems that are identified by their climax communities within a large geographical area having similar plants and animals as well as consistent climate

> **Terrestrial biomes:** biomes that cover land masses

> **Aquatic biomes:** biomes that are based within fresh or salt water

Ecosystem Ecology

Habitat: a description of the physical location of a population or community of organisms

Niche: a role or profession of an organism in its community and in ecology; includes its habitat combined with its behavior in that environment (i.e., range of conditions tolerated, methods of obtaining resources, number of offspring, time of reproduction, and all other environmental interactions for the organism)

> **Fundamental niche:** the range of conditions that a species can potentially tolerate and the range of resources it can potentially use

> **Realized niche:** the range of resources a species actually uses; this may vary based on competition or other interactions

Photoautotrophs: producers; green plants, algae, or cyanobacteria that convert light energy into food that can be consumed via photosynthesis

Chemoautotrophs: organisms that get their energy by consuming inorganic molecules (example: bacteria in sulfur springs or on hydrothermal vents)

Heterotrophs: consumers; obtain energy from food that they take into their bodies

Food chain: a simple model that scientists use to show how matter and energy move through an ecosystem; arrows in a food chain move in the direction of energy flow

Herbivores: consumers that feed directly on producers

Carnivores: consumers that feed directly on producers

Omnivores: consumers that eat both plants and animals; include humans, bears, raccoons, robins, etc.

Decomposers: saprotrophs; heterotroph consumers that get their energy by breaking down dead organisms without ingesting them

Trophic level: the position that an organism occupies in a food chain (example: primary consumers)

    Primary consumers: producers that use light directly

    Secondary consumers: herbivores that feed directly on plants

    Tertiary consumers: carnivores that feed on herbivores or other carnivores

Food web: a model that expresses all possible feeding relationships at each trophic level in a community

Biomass: the amount of dried, organic material in an organism

Ecological pyramids: illustrate the flow of energy, biomass, or numbers at each trophic level in an ecosystem; the highest level is the top of the food chain

    Pyramid of energy: illustrates the energy decrease at each trophic level

    Pyramid of numbers: illustrates the population size at each trophic level

    Pyramid of biomass: illustrates the biomass of living material at each trophic level

Primary productivity: the total amount of matter made by producers within an ecosystem

Water (hydrologic) cycle: the movement of water between different reservoirs on the earth, underground and in the atmosphere

Evaporation: process of liquid converting to the gaseous state

Transpiration: loss of water through stomata underneath leaves

Condensation: transition from a gas to a liquid as vapor condenses

Precipitation: the falling to earth of any form of water (rain, snow, hail, sleet, or mist)

Runoff: precipitation that is not absorbed or used which flows into lakes, etc.

Groundwater: water below the surface of the soil, between soil pores, and in rock spaces

Carbon cycle: process by which carbon in cycled through the biotic and abiotic environment in various chemical forms

Photosynthesis: process of converting light energy, carbon dioxide, and water into sugar and oxygen

Cellular respiration: process of using stored energy in food (such as sugar) along with oxygen into carbon dioxide and water

Decomposition: the slow breaking down of organic matter releasing carbon dioxide into the atmosphere; usually assisted by microorganisms or fungi

Deposition: transfer of organic carbon from the atmosphere to land: coal, petroleum, and calcium carbonate rock are deposited in sediment and underground; calcium carbonate deposits are eroded by water to form carbon dioxide; large amounts of carbon are tied up in wood, only returning to the atmosphere when wood is burned

Nitrogen cycle: process by which nitrogen is cycled through the biotic and abiotic environment in various chemical forms

Nitrogen fixation: the conversion of nitrogen gas (N_2) to ammonia (NH_3) by specific bacteria or lightning strikes; ammonia can be absorbed by plants from the soil and used to make proteins, thus entering the food web for consumers

Assimilation: occurs when consumers obtain nitrogen from the plants and animals they eat by digesting the food's proteins and using it to make their own proteins; plants assimilate nitrogen by absorbing nitrate (NO_2^-) or ammonium ions (NH_4^+) in the soil

Ammonification: occurs when decomposers return nitrogen from the remains of dead plants and animals back to the soil as ammonium (NH_4^+)

Denitrification: occurs when anaerobic bacteria (chemoautotrophs) break down nitrates (NO_3^-) and release nitrogen gas (N_2) back into the atmosphere

Nitrification: occurs when bacteria convert ammonia (NH_4^+) into nitrates (NO_3^-) that plants can utilize

Community Ecology

Competition: when organisms in same or different species attempt to use an ecological resource in the same place at the same time

Predation: an interaction in which one organism captures and feeds on another organism

Mutualism: symbiotic relationship where both species benefit

Commensalism: symbiotic relationship in which one member benefits and the other member is unaffected

Parasitism: symbiotic relationship in which one member benefits and the other member is harmed

Succession: a series of predictable changes in an ecosystem over time

Sere: each intermediate community that arises through succession

Primary succession: occurs where there has never been an ecosystem; for example – a volcano erupts, spreading lava

Secondary succession: the re-population of an area after is destruction due to natural or man-made causes

Pioneer species: the first species to colonize a new habitat; usually a lichen

Climax community: the community that will remain stable in a given area

Biodiversity: the number of different species in an ecosystem and how common each species is

Population Ecology

Geographic distribution (or range): the area inhabited by a population; can vary from a few cubic centimeters to millions of square kilometers

Population density: number of individuals in a population in a given area at a given time

Exponential growth: growth when individuals of a population reproduce at a constant rate without limiting factors; characterized by a J-curve (slow start, rapid and continuing increases)

Logistic growth: known as a realistic, slow growth curve that most populations exhibit because resources are limited; characterized by an S-curve (showing a lagging phase, an exponential phase, and then a slowing, logistic phase before settling down into its carrying capacity)

Carrying capacity: the maximum number of individuals that an ecosystem is capable of supporting; often represented by the symbol "K"

Limiting factors: conditions or events that may reduce the birth rate and/or increase the mortality rate

> **Density-dependent limiting factor:** a limiting factor that depends on population size

> **Density-independent limiting factor:** a limiting factor that does not depend on population size and is usually related to a natural event or disaster

R-strategist species: exploit less-crowded and unstable ecological niches and produce many offspring, each of which has a relatively low probability of surviving to adulthood

K-strategist species: strong competitors in crowded but stable niches and invest more heavily in fewer offspring, each of which has a relatively high probability of surviving to adulthood

Human Impact/Issues

Renewable resources: replaced or recycled by natural processes (examples: plants, animals, crops, soil, carefully managed water, wind, solar, geothermal power)

Nonrenewable resources: available only in limited amounts and not replaceable (examples: metals such as tin, silver, gold, uranium, and copper)

Greenhouse effect: natural process that traps heat in atmosphere; atmospheric gases (CO_2) act as an insulating blanket to trap heat and keep the earth from getting too cool at night; excess CO_2 may trap too much heat, resulting in global warming

Global warming: when the greenhouse effect is amplified by excess CO_2 in the atmosphere

Pollution: the contamination of soil, water, or air; results from human activity

Eutrophication: the addition of excess nutrients to a body of water, in many cases due to fertilizer runoff, that causes a bloom of producers; results in less oxygen, destroying other life in the body of water

Acid rain: air pollution containing sulfur oxides reacts with water vapor in the atmosphere to produce sulfuric acid which falls to the ground, damages crops, kills organisms in aquatic ecosystems, and erodes buildings and monuments; acid precipitation leaches calcium, potassium, and other valuable nutrients from the soil, making the soil less fertile

Biodegradable: wastes/object that can be broken down naturally by bacteria or other decomposers

Non-biodegradable: object/waste that stays in the environment for hundreds to thousands of years

Biological magnification (biomagnification; bioaccumulation): the increase in concentration of a chemical as trophic levels increase

Integrated pest management (IPM): an approach to reducing pests that considers all possible pest control techniques to minimize environmental impact and its effect upon human health

Ozone layer: high in the stratosphere, it protects Earth from U.V. radiation; O_2 molecules are converted into O_3 molecules to create ozone; some air pollutants can break down the ozone layer

Threatened: when population declines rapidly

Endangered: when numbers are so low that extinction is possible in the near future

Extinction: marks the end of the living members of any species

Invasive species (alien; introduced or non-native species): plant or animal species that is non-native to an area, yet has colonized and spread to the new location, causing damage ecologically, economically, or to human health; they typically have no natural control in the newer environment

Lesson 106: Biosphere Study Guide

1. What is ecology?

2. What does the biosphere contain?

3. Why do ecologists ask questions about events and organisms that range in complexity from an individual to the biosphere?

4. Complete the table about levels of organization.

Level	Definition
Species	
	A group of organisms that belong to the same species and live in the same area
Community	
Ecosystem	
	A group of ecosystems that have the same climate and dominant conditions

5. What is the highest level of organization that ecologists study?

6. What are the three basic approaches scientists use to conduct modern ecological research?

    1.

    2.

    3.

7. Why might an ecologist set up an artificial environment in a laboratory?

8. Why are many ecological phenomena difficult to study?

9. Why do ecologists make models?

10. Is the following sentence true or false? An ecological model may consist of a mathematical formula.

Lesson 107: Biomes Chart

Biome	Geographic Location	Climate: Rain and highs/lows	Major Types of Flora	Major Types of Fauna
Tundra				
Taiga (Coniferous Forest)				
Temperate (Deciduous Forest)				
Tropical Rainforest				
Shrubland (Chaparral)				
Grassland				
Desert				

Lesson 108: Energy Flow

autotroph	consumers	direct	eating	food
heterotrophs	indirect	organisms	producers	sun

An _____ is an organism that makes its own _____.

_____ are also called autotrophs. _____ are organisms

that get their energy by eating other _____. _____

are also called heterotrophs. All organisms get their energy from the

_____. Producers get _____ energy from the sun.

Consumers get _____ energy from the sun by _____

producers or other organisms that eat producers.

Lesson 112: Ocean Life

	Decomposer, Producer, or Consumer?	Eaten by...	Feeds on...	Other information
Zooplankton				
Seaweed				
Red cod				
Sea stars				
Phytoplankton				
Dolphins				
Crabs				
Cockles				
Arrow squid				
Bryozoans				
Sea birds				
Bacteria				
The sun				

1. a. Candy is hard.   Go to step 2

   b. Candy is not hard.   Go to step 5

2. a. Candy is spherical.   Go to step 3

   b. Candy is not spherical.   Go to step 4

3. a. Candy is on a stick.   *Coccus podus* _____

   b. Candy is not on a stick.   *Coccus tinus* _____

4. a. Candy has oblong shape.   *Bacillus frutus* _____

   b. Candy doesn't have oblong shape.   Go to step 6.

5. a. Candy is square.   *Esquandra frutus* _____

   b. Candy is not square.   Go to step 6.

6. a. Candy is flat.   Go to step 8.

   b. Candy is not flat.   Go to step 7.

7. a. Candy has oblong shape.   *Bacillus rollus* _____

   b. Candy doesn't have oblong shape.   *Pyramis bes* _____

8. a. Candy has 4 right angles.   *Rectiano verdus* _____

   b. Candy does not have right angles.   *Platys blancos* _____

Conclusions:

1. The scientific names are written as two words. This is called _____

   _____.

2. The first word is the _____.

3. The second word is the _____.

4. Use what you know about word origins and determine what platys means.

   _____

5. What do you think bacillus means? _____

6. Which one candy is missing? _____ Describe what that candy

   would look like and name a candy that fits those descriptions.

Lesson 150: Bacteria and Viruses Key Terms Biology with Lab

Microbes: things that are too small to be seen with the naked eye, including viruses and bacteria; many are also called germs or pathogens

Pathogen: disease-causing agent (virus, bacterium, protist, fungus)

Bacteria: one of two domains of prokaryotes; single-celled organisms that lack nuclei (singular: bacterium)

Virus: infectious agent composed of a core of DNA or RNA surrounded by a protein coat

Host: the organism that houses a disease-causing entity (bacteria, virus); the disease-causing entity would reproduce within the host (for example: you may be the host for *E. coli* if you have a stomach flu)

Viroid: plant pathogens; their genome is composed of very short, circular RNA

Prion: an infectious particle made of protein (rather than DNA or RNA) that has been misfolded; it may induce other proteins to fold in a similar manner to itself

Bacteria

Prokaryote: single-celled microorganism that lacks a nucleus; all bacteria

Archaebacteria: ancient forms of bacteria that survive extreme heat, acidity, salinity, or even methane

Eubacteria: slightly more advanced bacteria found in three common shapes: bacilli, cocci, and spirilla; range from mutualistic and beneficial forms to extremely deadly parasitic forms

Peptidoglycan: a polymer of sugars and amino acids which protects the cell from injury and determines its shape

Capsule: outer layer of some bacteria that protect them from drying out and being eaten

Pili: hairlike projections often used in bacterial conjugation; one type helps in motility (singular: pilus)

Nucleoid: bacteria genome (DNA)

Plasmid: tiny circular piece of DNA (separate from the bacterial genome) found in bacteria that typically contains antibiotic resistance genes or other genes beneficial to the bacteria

Flagellum: a whip-like structure that some prokaryotes (and eukaryotes) use for locomotion

Cocci: sphere-shaped bacterium (singular: coccus)

Bacilli: rod-shaped bacterium (singular: bacillus)

Spirilli: spiral/helical shaped bacterium (singular: spirillum)

Filamentous: elongated shape for a bacterium

Gram stain: technique for identifying eubacteria based on their cell wall structure; involves dyeing and rinsing the cells

Gram positive: bacteria with thick peptidoglycan layer that remain violet colored after gram staining

Gram negative: bacteria with thin peptidoglycan layer that remain red/pink colored after gram staining

Photoautotroph: organism that obtains energy directly from the sun

Chemoautotroph: organism that obtains energy directly from inorganic molecules

Photoheterotroph: a bacteria that is able to photosynthesize, but also requires organic compounds for nutrition

Taxes: movements toward or away from a stimulus (singular: taxis; phototaxis, hemotaxis, and magnetotaxis types exist in bacteria)

Obligate aerobes: organisms that require a constant supply of oxygen to live

Obligate anaerobes: organisms that do not require oxygen to live and can even be poisoned by it

Facultative anaerobes: organisms that do not require oxygen, but can switch between cellular respiration and fermentation; they can live anywhere!

Binary fission: asexual cell division in bacteria that results in two identical daughter cells (also occurs in some cell organelles such as mitochondria)

(bacterial) Conjugation: when a bacterium transfers genetic material (such as a plasmid) to another bacterium by physical contact with another cell; usually involves direct cell-to-cell contact and/or a bridge between cells

Endospore: tough, protective form of bacteria that is usually triggered by low-nutrient conditions; allows the bacteria to remain dormant until favorable conditions for growth arise

Pasteurization: a process of heating and cooling food products repeatedly so that the endospores which break out of dormancy into regular bacterial form during cooling will be killed if heated again

Sterilization: any effective means of removing or killing pathogens; it may involve using heat, chemicals, irradiation, or pressure

Antibiotic: compound that kills or stops the growth and reproduction of bacteria

Zones of inhibition (ZOI): in bacterial culture, an area where bacteria are not growing because a chemical agent (like an antibiotic) is inhibiting their growth

Bioremediation: a process where bacteria are used to clean up waste water or oil spills or to convert garbage to compost

Nitrogen fixation: the process of converting nitrogen gas into a chemical form that plants can use

Viruses

Capsid: the outer boundary of a virus, composed of protein

Retrovirus: virus that stores its genetic information as RNA

Bacteriophage: virus that infects bacteria

Lytic (lytic cycle): type of viral reproduction or infection in which the viral cell releases its DNA into the host cell and the host cell makes new viruses by reading viral DNA; the host cell bursts, releasing the manufactured viruses; viruses that use the lytic cycle are called virulent

Lysis: process of breaking apart or bursting a cell

Lysogenic (lysogenic cycle): type of viral reproduction or infection in which the host cell integrates copies of the viral DNA within its own genome and the viral DNA is copied into daughter cells as part of normal bacterial reproduction; the host cell does not lyse; viruses that use the lysogenic cycle are called temperate because they do not immediately cause disease

Interferon: a protein produced by cells when exposed to a virus; this protein binds to the cell membranes of neighboring cells and "interferes" with the ability of a virus to enter the cell

Vaccine: part of a virus (or bacterium) that has been permanently damaged or *attenuated* (weakened) used to prevent infection by exposing a host to it; its role is to stimulate the body's immune system so that it destroys and then records information about the invader, should it return again.

Kingdom Protista

Endosymbiont Theory: theory that explains the origins of some eukaryotic organelles (mitochondria, chloroplasts) as the result of a symbiosis between a free-living prokaryote and a primitive eukaryotic cell

Animal-like protists (Protozoa): mostly unicellular and motile heterotrophs that are obligate aquatic organisms (require water)

Pseudopodia: temporary projections of the cell membrane and cytoplasm that extend and retract to allow for movement and food ingestion in Amoeboid cells (example: Amoeba)

Amoeboid movement: type of movement in some Protozoa resulting from the use of pseudopodia

Cilia: packed rows of short, hair-like structures extending from the cell membrane that assist in movement example: Paramecium)

Flagella: long, hair-like structure that extends from the cell membrane, assisting in movement; more than one may be present (example: Euglena)

Sporozoan: protozoan that is not motile (stationary)

Pellicle: protective coating outside the cell membrane present in some Protozoa (example: Euglena)

Contractile vacuole: an organelle in some Protozoa that expands and contracts to regulate water balance with the environment

Eyespot (stigma): an organelle in some protists that has photoreceptors, allowing the organism to detect light direction and intensity (example: Chlamydomonas or Euglena)

Plant-like protists (algae): photoautotrophs without roots, stems, or leaves; may be unicellular, multicellular, or colonial; obligate aquatic organisms

Phytoplankton: microscopic photosynthetic organisms that float near the surface of the water and serve as the basis for food in aquatic food chains

Red tide: a type of algal bloom (population explosion) of phytoplankton (usually Dinoflagellates) that turns the water brown or red; they are generally harmful to the ecosystem and can result in toxins released and low oxygen in the water

Eutrophication: an excess of fertilizer in a body of water causing an algal bloom that depletes the water of oxygen, therefore killing other life

Spores: reproductive structures that are the result of meiosis and contain half the normal chromosome number (they are haploid)

Fungus-like protists: heterotrophs that absorb their nutrients rather than ingesting food; groups include the slime molds and the water molds

Kingdom Fungi

Chitin: a complex polysaccharide in the cell walls of fungi; also found in the exoskeleton of insects

Hyphae: the thin, vegetative filaments of Fungi; one cell layer in thickness (singular: hypha)

Mycelium: a mass of hyphae; may form a tangled mat (example: bread mold) or an organized body (example: pizza mushroom) (singular: mycelia)

Fruiting body: reproductive structures of Fungi, composed of mycelia supporting spore-producing structures (such as basidia or asci)

Saprobe: a heterotrophic organism that lives on dead and decaying organic matter by absorbing rather than ingesting it

Ectomycorrhizal fungi: microscopic soil fungi that penetrate the cells of plant roots – a relationship that may be beneficial to both parties or may be harmful to the plant; they grow thick coats of mycelia around the rootlets of trees and bring water and minerals from the soil into the roots; in return, the host tree supplies the fungus with sugars, vitamins, and other root substances.

Lichens: a symbiosis (mutualism) between a fungus and either a green alga or photosynthetic bacteria

Fragmentation: a means of asexual reproduction in Fungi when hyphae are physically separated from each other; the parts regenerate and can continue living

Budding: process of yeast asexual reproduction where the original yeast cell pinches itself off to produce a small offspring cell

Spores: microscopic, non-motile cells that serve as asexual reproduction in Fungi; can develop into a new organism

Sporangia: structures that produce spores (singular: sporangium)

Septa: internal cell walls within the hyphae; often contain holes that allow organelles and other items to pass among the hyphae (singular: septum)

Coenocytic: containing more than one nucleus; mycelia without septa would be coenocytic

Ascus (sac): structure that produces spores in Orange Cup fungi

Basidia: structures that produce spores in mushrooms (singular: basidium)

Virtual Pond Dip

Name	Unicellular or Multicellular	Size	Where to find it	Detailed Description	Food source (autotroph or heterotroph)	Special adaptation	Unique fact	Classification (Kingdom, phylum, and class)

Lesson 166: Fungi Notes Biology with Lab

Introduction to the Kingdom Fungi

1. Are Fungi eukaryotes or prokaryotes?

2. Where are Fungi found (habitat)?

3. What size are fungi?

4. Why are fungi vital for life on Earth?

5. What is a **mycologist**?

6. List the basic characteristics of all Fungi here:

7. To which other eukaryotic Kingdom are Fungi more closely related?

Fungal Structure

8. Describe features of Fungal cell wall:

Lesson 166: Fungi Notes (cont.)

9. Define the three structures that make up most Fungi. Sketch a picture of each.

Structure	Definition/Explanation	Sketch
Hyphae		
Mycelium		
Fruiting body		

Fungal Nutrition

10. Do fungi have chloroplasts?

11. For each of the four modes of nutrition mentioned, jot down a few examples.

Mode of Nutrition	Explanation	Examples:
Decomposer/Saprobe		
Parasite/Pathogen		
Symbioses		
Predators		

Lesson 166: Fungi Notes (cont.)

Fungal Reproduction

12. List the 3 ways in which Fungi sexually reproduce:

1.

2.

3.

13. All sexual reproduction in Fungi involves _____.

Fungal Life Cycle

14. Annotate the diagram below to describe a Fungus' life from spore to fruiting body:

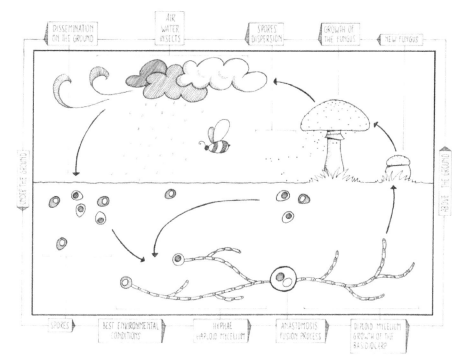

Lesson 166: Fungi Notes (cont.)

Classification of Fungi

15. Complete the table below to organize your thoughts from reading about the taxonomic groups of Fungi:

Division (Phylum)	Examples	General Features	Sexual structures unique to this Division
Zygomycota			
Ascomycota			
Basidiomycota			
Deuteromycota			

16. What is a Lichen?

17. Describe at least one way in which lichens are important ecologically:

Beneficial Fungi

18. Give an example of how the Fungi are beneficial in each of these areas:

- Economically –

- Medically –

- Ecologically -

Harmful Fungi

19. Give an example of how the Fungi are harmful in each of these ways:

- Economically –

- Medically –

- Ecologically -

	Porifera	Cnidaria	Platyhelminthes	Nematoda
Special Features of this Phylum				
Body Plan: Symmetry and Coelom Type				
Feeding (Digestive System)				
Movement (Muscular System)				
Respiration/ Gas Exchange (Respiratory System)				
Circulatory System (if present, open or closed?)				
Excretion (removal of waste)				
Sensory and Response (Nervous System)				
Reproduction (a/sexual, hermaphrodite)				
Example groups, or organisms:				

Lesson 173: Animal Phyla Fact Sheet (cont.)   Biology with Lab

	Annelida	Mollusca	Arthropoda	Echinodermata	Chordata
Special Features of this Phylum					
Body Plan: Symmetry and Coelom Type					
Feeding (Digestive System)					
Movement (Muscular System)					
Respiration/ Gas Exchange (Respiratory System)					
Circulatory System (if present, open or closed?)					
Excretion (removal of waste)					
Sensory and Response (Nervous System)					
Reproduction (a/sexual, hermaphrodite)					
Example groups, or organisms:					

Made in the USA
Coppell, TX
21 July 2025

52151461R00063